Preface

Welcome to "The Secret Garden of Bright Flower." I am Ty Bright Flower, and I invite you to embark on a journey that delves into the depths of spiritual enlightenment. This book is not for everyone. It is crafted for those who have advanced far along their spiritual path, seeking more understanding and connection.

The writings in this book are not mere words, but poetic expressions that have the power to transform your consciousness. Each poem is a contemplative tool, inviting you to meditate on each concept and allowing the wisdom to permeate your being.

Within these pages, you will explore the mysteries of the third eye, the intricate dance of the ego and spirit, and the power of the word as a sound frequency. These concepts, drawn from my experiences as an Ordained Mystic with Spiritual Humanism, I reflect a forward-thinking, enlightened approach to spirituality.

As you delve into these pages, I invite you to not just read, but to experience. The spirit resides within each of us, transcending the boundaries of individuality. This book is an invitation to experience that truth, to see with the eye of the spirit, and to embrace the light within.

May "The Secret Garden of Bright Flower" serve as a guide and inspiration on your continued journey towards spiritual awakening and enlightenment.

Ty Bright Flower

For my husband Victor and children, George, Annalyse, Adam, Sean, Marcus, Alex, and Victor II, and my grandchildren, Anastaysia, Nataliya, Jenavieve, Caius, and Atlas

The Secret Garden of Bright Flower

Anthology

Tyrese Gould Jacinto

Art by Arnild C. Aldepolla

Table

Enlightened Eye

In the air where delicate whispers sow,

A vision unfolds, a cosmic mystic flow.

The vibration of "I" and the gaze of the eye,

Merge in resonance, as awakened spirits abide.

Eternal echoes, a dance of being,

"I am" vibrates, the soul's decreeing.

Lights eye, a solitary keeper in the dark,

Unveils the mysteries and leaves its marks.

The ego, a shadow in the cosmic place,

Lost in illusions, yearning for space.

Yet rest beyond the veil, a radiant light,

Awakens the soul in celestial spite.

Ancient tales spin of this sacred haze,

Where wisdom resides, in mystical daze.

Within us it stirs, its essence divine,

Guiding our way through the cosmic design.

Our eyes surrender with revelation, anew,

And witness beholds, in the cosmic hue.

A vessel of light, in celestial embrace,

Awakening the truth, an infinite grace.

Beating of the heart, a path now unfolds,

Where green light pulses, the stories untold.

Heart is the center, where love's roots do reach,

In a cosmic symphony, all truths beseech.

Green disappears in renewal and birth,

In its silent presence, all merge in earth.

In our heart's core, our mysteries reside,

As love's eternal song, and it fills the sky.

We heed this decree, in the cosmic abide,

"I" is transformed into the sands of our time.

For no longer "I" abides, you will see,

But the cosmos within, we are forever free.

With threads of mystic whispers weave,

A tapestry sound so profound we breathe.

"I" and "eye," an ancient sound,

Merge as one, where songs are found.

Ehyeh, the echo of existence divine,

"I am" whispers, in the sacred design.

Ayin, the Eye, in its singular gaze,

Unveils the secrets, in its mystical haze.

The eye, the ego, in its shadowed lore,

Seeks itself, in illusions endure.

Yet single eye waves, radiant and bright,

Beyond the veil, in the eternal light.

Our ancestors tell of this sacred sight,

The unspoken wisdom, of shining light.

Within us it lies, the Creator's own breath,

Guiding us through our life as we set.

With ego's surrender, our visions anew,

Single the eye, to the mystical taboo.

Vessels of light, in celestial dance,

Awakening to the truth, in our cosmic prance.

The secrete whispers, a journey to the heart,

Where green light pulses, as mystical art.

Right in the center, where love finds its beat,

In galactic harmony, where all vibrations meet.

As green is the hue and the reverse is the light,

With its invisible glow, all truths are in sight.

Our heart's core, where mysteries unfold,

Vibrates eternal songs, in whispers untold.

We embrace this decree, in mystical rhyme,

"I" transformed into the veil of our time.

For no longer "I" resides, you see,

But the Universe is within, we are forever free.

The dance of frequencies, as words transcend,

A vision unfolded, a message we send.

"I" and "eye," entwined in their sound,

Echoing truths in vibrations profound.

Ehyeh, we hear, the whispers of beings,

"I am" is vibrating with those who are seeing.

Ayin, our eye, in its singular state,

Unveiling mysteries, sealing our fate.

The eyes, the ego, no longer the story,

No tale of separateness or seeking the glory.

The light internal, our consciousness is pure,

The death of the ego, our ultimate cure.

Ancestors sing of this singular sight,

Where within we find wisdom, radiant light.

Within us it dwells, the Creator's own spark,

Guiding us all throughout the dark.

With ego's demise, our vision reborn,

Singular eye, to the light we sworn.

Vessels of light, we in this new of grace,

Awakened to truth, in our sacred space.

Internal lights whisper, a path to the heart,

Where little sparks dance, a symphony to start.

With all acceptance, In the balance it lies,

Perfect harmony, a rhythmic collide.

In the tapestry entwined, we are colorful strands,

As human beings, wrapped in spiritual hands.

Our existence an essence, a spark of divine light,

Is guiding us through our consciousness flight.

In this earthly vessel, we dance, and we weave,

As spiritual beings, dressed in human sleeves.

We are enlightened spirits, in mortal attire,

Leading our life's journey, earth, water, and fire.

We as awakened souls, embark on our humanity,

Embracing our vessel with conscious sanity.

For our body is a temple, a sacred space,

A vessel for the spirit's divine earthly grace.

Enlightened eye, we see the intertwined,

Our threads of life, in vibration aligned.

Every being, every creature, and every tree,

A reflection of us in divine unity.

We rejoice in the earthly spirit delight,

Honoring each moment, in the dance of light.

As mindful of our spiritual roots,

In the depths of our souls, where heart takes root.

So as we cherish this earthly sojourn,

A journey of spirit, where experiences are born.

For in this union of spirit and flesh,

Lies the essence of life's magical mesh.

As peaceful our transformation, we surrender,

Asleep to the flesh, in spirit's tender.

Born anew in the realm of the divine,

Our essence, a vessel for mystical design.

The vessel, a beautiful shell, not so frail,

And within them, the spirits can prevail.

As we shed the old, we embrace the new,

In the cosmic dance, our dreams come true.

Empty vessels, we stand in the mystical glow,

Awaiting the whispers, the spirit to flow.

For our spirit, a collective thought divine,

A symphony of vibrations, in the light shrine.

We are but channels, conduits of the will,

Empty vessels, in deep silence, and still.

Filled and emptied, by the hand of fate,

Guided by the Creator, in timeless space.

In this sacred dance, we find our place,

A vessel of love, in the mystical trace.

For in emptiness, lies the divine plan,

A canvas for creation, in the palm of the hand.

So let us surrender, to the will inside,

Empty vessels, in the mystical divine.

For in emptiness, we find our true worth,

A vessel for love, in the Creators' birth.

It's No longer I, But the Creator That Lives In Me

For three decades, I held onto the biblical verse, "It is no longer I that lives, but the Creator that lives in me." Little did I know that this phrase would unlock the mysteries of consciousness in a prophetic dream.

In my dream, I was shown the profound connection between the "I" and the "eye," a revelation transcending linguistic and cultural barriers. In Hebrew, "I" resonates as "ehyeh," while the "eye" corresponds to "ayin," both sharing the same sound frequency. "ehyeh" also translates to "I am," hinting at a deeper understanding of the self.

Often associated with the ego, self-awareness, and selfishness, the eye took on a new significance as I delved into ancient texts. Here, it was portrayed as the pineal gland, or the third eye, an organ of light consciousness and the death of the ego. With this transformation, our eyes cease to be separate entities but become vessels solely for the Third Eye, embodying the essence of "I am."

Located at the center of our vision, the pineal gland leads us inward, towards the heart. Symbolized by green, the heart represents the balance between love and hate, which is acceptance. It is the nexus of all spectrums, both in light and sound frequencies, embodying the interconnectedness of all beings.

In embracing our spiritual journey, we transcend the limitations of the flesh, being reborn in the spirit. We become vessels for the collective thought, empty yet receptive to the will of the Creator.

Through this enlightenment, we find harmony in our humanity, caring for our bodies while remaining aware of our interconnected existence.

As human beings, we are not merely flesh and bone but vessels for a higher purpose a purpose that unfolds as we surrender to the divine within us.

Cohanzick, We Are

In Lenapehoking, our waters do wind,

Cohanzick, we are, with our spirits entwined.

Though ancient soil, our stories still grow,

We keep this land, our ancient wisdom that flows.

Cohanzick, we are, our ancestral wise,

In its currents, lies our wisdom resides.

Each drink we take, with the water embrace,

Have the ancestors whisper, in every drop we taste.

The past and present flow, in our bloodstream,

Our bodies of water, a vessel esteemed,

As the river's guardians, a legacy is true,

As seven generations, the future, we pass through.

From the depths of water, to the rivers that wind,

An unbroken circle, our legacy defined.

Cohanzick, we are, in time's endless stance,

Our river's name is etched, on each watery trance.

In our marshes and meadows, our whispers unfold,

Cohanzick, we are, a tale true and old.

As seven generations pass, a circle of time,

In the river's flow, each is a part of the climb.

In the shadows of cedars, where ancestors abide,

Our Cohanzick spirits, smoke as an eternal guide.

The river's veins sing, the stories of old,

A story of resilience, seven generations of bold.

Our roots in the soil, our connection so deep,

Cohanzick, we are, a promise we keep.

In the glow of the moon, on the water's face,

A reflection of us, we are bound by fate.

We are the future, we stand, unbroken space,

Living with the rivers, where ancestors' pace.

In the flow of the current, in a timeless trance,

Cohanzick, we are, in a seven-generation expanse.

Cohanzick, we are, a whisper in the breeze,

Carried by currents, in valleys and trees.

We are past, present, future, entwined in river's flow,

Seven generations of existence, in a steady growth.

In the silent whisper, of the Cohanzick's flow,

Steps of our ancestors, seven generations did sow.

Each current, a circle of our people's tale,

A living connection, and spirits prevail.

With reverence, we sip from nature's embrace,

A mix of ancestors of past, present, and future, we face.

The river's lifeblood, atop the land,

Cohanzick, we are, and tall as we stand.

Capturing the Spirit of
Cohanzick People

In celebration of the symbiotic connection to my land and the spirits that reside within it, I offer a glimpse into the people of the Cohanzick waters. Through the lens of my collective heritage, we embody the essence of the Cohanzick River, ponds, and streams, the story of the timeless beauty that has echoed through the ages.

Envision the whispers of my ancestors dancing through the winding curves of our Cohanzick waters. Each is a testament to the enduring dance between water and life, mirroring the journey of our Indigenous families whose footsteps have left an incredible mark on this sacred landscape.

Feel the reflections of our shared past, the shimmering waters embodying the stories passed down through generations. The ponds and streams carry the vibrations of laughter, the rustle of leaves, and the gentle flow of time, resonating with the harmony that binds us to the earth.

Feel the vibration of water as it feeds the flora and fauna of our families that call the Cohanzick home. Each is a testament to the resilience of our consciousness, a stark reminder of the sacred symbiosis between our humanity and the natural world.

Imagine each as a bridge between the past, present, and the promise of the future. May the Cohanzick River, ponds, and streams inspire a sense of responsibility for us to protect and cherish this sacred land, ensuring its beauty for the next seven generations and beyond.

Individual Coincidence

It's a coincidence; you are an individual.

Your intention resulted from your attention,

in cooperation with the indivisible.

This led you to your production,

which is a coincidence.

Your attention led to your intention,

to cooperate with the indivisible.

This led you to your destruction,

which is a coincidence,

you are an individual,

in cooperation with the indivisible.

Your attention will always guide you,

to your intention, this must be,

in cooperation with the indivisible,

to bring you your production or destruction

for you are an individual.

You are intentional and coincidental,

An individual in cooperation with the indivisible.

What's In A Word? – Thoughts!

The term "intention" refers to the inner nature or quality of something to denote a concept or idea's inherent characteristics or properties.

"In" refers to a state of being within or connected to something, suggesting a state of unity or alignment with the Creator. It implies a sense of being intertwined or unified with a greater whole.

"Tension" refers to a state of pressure arising from forces or tendencies. In the context of thoughts and manifestation, tension signifies the dynamic interplay between mental states, desires, and external factors that influence the process of bringing thoughts or intentions into reality.

So, combining these interpretations, "intension" implies a state of inner alignment or connection with the Creator characterized by the dynamic interplay of thoughts and desires being pulled towards manifestation.

"Attention" can be broken down into two words: "At" Refers to a point in space, time, or situation. "Tension" Signifies a state of strain or pressure.

So, "attention" implies a state of inner alignment or connection with the Creator, characterized by the dynamic interplay of thoughts and desires being pulled towards manifestation.

Cooperation means being one with the Creator in the process of bringing about manifestation with the Creator.

"Co" Refers to joint or mutual action, implying unity or alignment with the Creator. "Operation" is the process or series of actions to achieve a particular goal or outcome.

So, when these words are combined, "cooperation" is understood as the joint effort or coordinated action towards a shared goal or manifestation, implying alignment with the Creator.

Breaking down coincidence, "Co" signifies unity or alignment with the Creator, suggesting a connection to a higher power or purpose.

"Incidence" refers to the occurrence or outcome of a particular thought, desire, or manifestation, implying the result or effect of a specific event or situation.

Looking at "coincidence" through this lens suggests a synchronicity or alignment between one's actions, desires, or thoughts and the unfolding of events in the external world. It implies a sense of harmony or resonance with the Creator, where unrelated occurrences converge meaningfully.

Production is the steady thought of manifestation and one with the Creator.

"Pro" the prefix denotes forward movement, advancement, or prior to.

"duction" is associated with the root "duct," which refers to leading or guiding.

Combining these interpretations, "production" is understood as the process of advancing or leading towards manifestation, suggesting a sense of alignment or unity with the Creator in the steady thought and realization of goals or outcomes. It implies an active role in achieving desired results, guided by an inner sense of purpose or connection to a greater source.

Destruction blocks the manifestation instead of producing results in cooperation with the Creator. Breaking down "destruction" into two parts according to our interpretation:

"De" prefix often denotes reversal, negation, or removal.

"Struction" relates to building or creating something.

Combining these interpretations, "destruction" is understood as reversing or negating the creation or manifestation, indicating a blocking or hindering of results in contrast to cooperation with the Creator. It implies actions or forces that dismantle or obstruct the realization of desired outcomes, opposing the forward movement or alignment with the Creator inherent in production.

Indivisible means one with the Creator, divisible means together with the Creator; visible is being aware as the Creator.

Breaking down "indivisible" and "divisible."

"In" this prefix suggests negation or not.

"Divisible" capable of being divided or separated into parts.

Combining these interpretations, "indivisible" is understood as not being able to be divided or separated from the Creator, implying a sense of oneness or unity with the divine or higher power.

Additionally, "divisible" suggests the ability to be divided or separated from the Creator, indicating a state where one is not fully aligned or united with the divine source. The "devil," "divide," the "dual eye," and the ego.

Regarding "visible"

"Vis" refers to sight or perception.

"Ible" Denoting capability or potential.

So, when we consider 'visible' in a spiritual context, it takes on a whole new depth. It signifies the potential to perceive or be aware of the Creator, indicating an awareness of one's unity or connection with the divine source. It's about the ability to perceive the divine within oneself and the world around them, a concept symbolized by the third eye.

Individual as "in," "divi," and "dual" is one with the Creator and is a dual spiritual thinking manifestation.

Breaking down "individual" into three parts

"In" meaning being within or connected to.

"Divi" suggesting divinity or being one with the Creator.

"Dual" refers to having two aspects or components.

Combining these interpretations, "individual" is understood as a being who is within or connected to the divine or the Creator, implying a sense of spiritual unity or alignment. Additionally, the inclusion of "dual" suggests that this individual embodies both earthly and divine aspects, representing a dualistic spiritual nature.

Therefore, an individual, in this sense, is the manifestation of spiritual enlightenment that encompasses both material and divine elements. We are one with the Creator. Spiritual beings having human experiences.

Epilogue

The poems and explanations can be described by the idea that vibrations as words and thoughts are magical or have power. Words and thoughts can influence reality, so exploring the concept in terms of sound and thought frequencies is interesting.

Imagine if we were to view all words and imagination as frequencies. This perspective takes us into the realm of spirit and its profound influence on our psyche and environment. Frequency, a potent force, has the capacity to stir emotions, create resonance, and even shape physical matter through phenomena like resonance and vibration.

Each word carries its unique frequency, which can vary depending on pronunciation, intonation, context, and concentration. Our ancestors believe certain sounds or vibrations have specific resonating qualities that can bring about desired effects, like healing, transformation, or manifestation.

The power of spoken vibration is in its ability to convey meaning, evoke emotions, and shape perception. In this sense, the idea of "spelling" can be seen metaphorically as weaving blessings using vibrations of thought to influence consciousness and reality.

The awe-inspiring nature of vibrations is found in their ability to inspire, persuade, and communicate complex ideas, emotions, and intentions. It's in the subtle whispers of these vibrations, and their mystical properties, that we find ourselves captivated and fascinated.

Vibrations are formed from the breath of the inner consciousness, which cannot be seen, lies within the heart, and leads to the eternal internal eye we know as the Creator!

Thank you,

Ty Bright Flower